T0150964

category e
belinda cornish

playwrights canada press
toronto

LIBRARY AND ARCHIVES CANADA CATALOGUING IN PUBLICATION
Title: Category E / by Belinda Cornish.
Names: Cornish, Belinda, author.
Description: First edition. | A play.
Identifiers: Canadiana (print) 20190055618 | Canadiana (ebook) 20190055707 |
ISBN 9781770919785 (softcover) | ISBN 9781770919792 (PDF) |
ISBN 9781770919808 (EPUB) | ISBN 9781770919815 (Kindle)
Classification: LCC PS8605.O7675 C38 2019 | DDC C812/.6—dc23

Playwrights Canada Press acknowledges that we operate on land, which, for thousands of years, has been the traditional territories of the Mississaugas of the Credit First Nation, Huron-Wendat, Anishinaabe, Métis, and Haudenosaunee peoples. Today, this meeting place is home to many Indigenous peoples from across Turtle Island and we are grateful to have the opportunity to work and play here.

We acknowledge the financial support of the Canada Council for the Arts—which last year invested $153 million to bring the arts to Canadians throughout the country—the Ontario Arts Council (OAC), Ontario Creates, and the Government of Canada for our publishing activities.

For Atom

foreword
by ruth bratt

What are we supposed to care about? There are so many demands on our compassion, it's hard to know. There's plastic in the ocean; the orangutans are being killed for palm oil; if we don't use palm oil we condemn the people who farm it to poverty; there's a refugee crisis; homelessness is visibly on the rise; chicken is being washed with chlorine; cows are being fed hormones. It's hard not to get empathy fatigue. It's also hard to know whose side to be on—as feminists and trans activists clash, as animal-rights charities disagree amongst themselves, as charities that campaign for human rights admit to a culture of bullying within their own organizations.

In 1990 it was pretty simple. Maybe because I was fourteen. Maybe because there was no internet. It was pretty much all about ending animal cruelty, freeing Nelson Mandela, and saving the planet, wasn't it? I was obsessed with these three things. I'd already given up pig-meat products when my primary school thought an appropriate field trip for a group of seven-year-olds was a visit to the local butcher to make sausages. It was like *The Texas Chainsaw Massacre*. No more sausages. Then I discovered the Body Shop and Anita Roddick and my eyes were opened. I gave up meat; I only bought cruelty-free products. I did my talk for English class on battery farming and vivisection. I had posters all over my walls, not of Keanu Reeves or River Phoenix, but about sustainability, recycling, feminism, and the evils of the fur trade (the slogans of which I now realize often directly contradicted one another—"It takes forty dumb bitches to make this coat, but only one to wear it."—eeesh.)

I dreamt of being one of those activists who broke into research facilities—especially after watching an episode of *Casualty*—the UK version of *ER*, only a lot less gritty, a lot less pretty, but remarkably durable—in which some animal-rights bods did exactly that, but got bitten by the ungrateful animals and ended up in Emergency. I was desperate for some direct action.

But in suburban London in 1990 there wasn't much chance of that. I mooched about the high street because there wasn't much to do in Orpington other than hang around outside McDonald's, hang around outside the Civic Centre, hang around outside the Walnuts Leisure Centre, or sign a new petition every weekend—you know the ones, with all the graphic images of abused, tortured animals. So I did that.

And my petitioning worked. It became illegal to test cosmetics on animals! The EU banned battery-farmed chickens in 1999! I could relax and use all the products! I hit my thirties, got hungry and apathetic and started eating meat again.

But then . . .

A few years ago I was working on a puppet show and was asked to sing a song, as a cow, for the World Animal Protection campaign to prevent mega-dairies from being built in the UK. What now? MEGA-dairies? I thought these things were illegal . . . once again my eyes were opened. And I suddenly saw all the loopholes. And for me, some of the most saddening and infuriating were the ones about animal testing.

Cosmetic testing is still illegal in the UK. But it's not everywhere else. And in some countries it's COMPULSORY. What now? And of course, some of the brands of makeup that I was blithely using sell their products in some of these markets. So I was no longer living a cruelty-free lifestyle. And then you look further into it. Oh, god, the cleaning products I used, the medicines I took, the deodorant I used . . . so I found an online resource (crueltyfreekitty.com) that tells you whether a brand is cruelty free or not (it's bloody brilliant, check it out). I do as much campaigning as I can for World Animal Protection, but is it enough? And when people are worried about people, how can we ask them to be worried about animals? And when people don't seem to care about people, how can we get them to care about animals?

Belinda's play is one way how. I sent her an email when I read it saying, "Your play is FANTASTIC" (except I used some more profane words for emphasis!). And it is. I read it so fast because I couldn't stop. And I was invested from the first second. It's funny and painful and hilarious and gross and provoking, and all the things that aren't easy. When we look at how easy it is to dehumanize actual humans, as refugees are painted as a seething mass of danger rather than people trying to escape from horror, it's an edifying thing to read a play about humans being treated like animals.

By humanizing the animals, turning them into actual humans, Belinda is asking us to empathize in a world where empathy can feel like a shrinking commodity. And by empathizing with these humans, perhaps we can see why it is wrong to treat animals in this way. And maybe we can prevent humans being treated like animals, because there is a line, one we can follow, where lack of empathy leads to lack of empathy leads to lack of empathy leads to . . .

No one can be expected to care about everything. No one can be expected to do all of the things. But we can all do one thing. Or two things. And we also don't have to KNOW THE ANSWER. We don't have to be didactic. It's okay to be ambivalent. It's okay to be unsure. It's okay to say, "I don't agree with cosmetic testing, but what about medical experimentation?" and then try to find the answers for yourself. This play invites you to ask those questions. Be inquisitive. Don't just accept that this is the way it is. Find out the answers for yourself. And listen to narratives that aren't your narrative. The world seems to be polarizing (I write this as the UK is dealing with Brexit, and whatever side of that debate you're on, we can all agree it's a pretty divisive one, with no outcome that will satisfy everyone), and part of that polarization has to do with a lack of debate, and echo chambers. Learn how to debate.

Hear the other side. You don't have to agree, but try to hear. And know that some things, like makeup and deodorant, are not worth compromising your humanity for.

Ruth Bratt is a writer/performer/improviser. As an improviser, she is a regular guest with the Comedy Store Players; is one quarter of the Glenda J Collective with Josie Lawrence, Pippa Evans, and Cariad Lloyd; one half of *A Very Serious Play* with Lee Simpson; is often in *The Actor's Nightmare*; and has guested on *Whose Line Is It Anyway Live*. She is a founding member of *Showstopper! The Improvised Musical*, with whom she has performed and taught all over the world, as they continue to tour worldwide and perform regularly in the West End following their Olivier Award–winning run in 2015. She's a regular player in the London 50-hour Improvathons, and has done two with Die-Nasty in Edmonton, where it all started! She plays Roche in the BAFTA-winning show *People Just Do Nothing* (BBC), and was Carol in the last series of *Man Down* for Channel 4. She wrote and performed *Trodd En Bratt Say Well Done You* with Lucy Trodd (BBC Radio 4). Other credits include *Derek* (C4), *Mongrels* (BBC 3), and *Sarah Millican's Support Group* (Radio 4). Ruth is an ambassador for World Animal Protection, and likes sitting on sofas with dogs and cats, and is obsessed with ceramics and becoming a part-time potter.

Category E was first produced by The Maggie Tree at the Varscona Theatre, Edmonton, from April 10 to 18, 2015, with the following cast and creative team:

Millet: Miranda Allen
Corcoran: Louise Lambert
Filigree: Jenna Dykes-Busby

Director: Nancy McAlear
Stage Manager: Erin Valentine
Production and Media Design: ShowStages Collective
Producers: Kristi Hansen and Vanessa Sabourin

The play was first produced in Toronto at the Coal Mine Theatre from April 11 to 29, 2018, with the following cast and creative team:

Millet: Vivien Endicott-Douglas
Corcoran: Robert Persichini
Filigree: Diana Bentley

Director: Rae Ellen Bodie
Set and Costume Design: Anna Treusch
Lighting Design: Gabriel Cropley
Sound Design: Keith Thomas

characters

Corcoran: Forties to sixties. Tired, laconic, wry. Curmudgeonly. It only has the use of one eye and is in a wheelchair. One or more limbs are bandaged. For the information of the actor and director, please see the Draize eye test, similar tests for chemical reactions on abraded skin, and spinal fractures in improperly restrained test rabbits.

Millet: Twenties to thirties. Gregarious and friendly, with youthful punchy energy. For the information of the actor and director, please see vitamin K–antagonist poisoning (e.g., brodifacoum) and symptoms of hypovolemic shock.

Filigree: Should read as young. Impetuous, driven by creature curiosity. For the information of the actor and director, please see "knockout mouse," Harry Harlow's social isolation experiments on rhesus monkeys (the "Well of Despair"), and nephrectomies and their accompanying scarring.

The characters are never referred to by gender and can by played by anyone.

If helpful for clarity, the category designations may be described with the phonetic alphabet: Alpha, Bravo, Charlie, Delta, and Echo.

In the first production, these designations were also projected onto a screen.

punctuation notes

Forward slash (/): the next person's line overlaps at the point.

Em dash (—): the line cuts off.

Ellipsis (. . .): the line trails off.

Brackets around a line indicate the idea of the line, which is usually not spoken.

Category E: procedures causing severe pain near, at, or above the pain tolerance threshold of unanesthetized conscious animals; procedures causing unrelieved pain and stress due to the scientific end point being death.

—Canadian Council on Animal Care (CCAC)
policy on invasiveness of procedures
in animal science

A simple, clean room. Two cots and a small table and two chairs. A little shelving unit with board games. A security camera in one corner. There are two people in the room— CORCORAN and FILIGREE. FILIGREE is young and coltish and currently asleep on one of the cots. CORCORAN is older, sitting in a wheelchair, something terribly wrong with one of its eyes. They are dressed in white, each with a number stitched on the left breast—455743 for FILIGREE, 622149 for CORCORAN.

CORCORAN appears to be doing the crossword. Its hand absent-mindedly creeps to its face and starts to scratch at its eye with increasing enthusiasm until suddenly—pain. CORCORAN winces and pulls its hand away. It examines the something that came off its face, stuck under its nail. Peers at it. Sniffs it. Sneezes. Flicks the something away. Returns to the crossword.

The door opens. MILLET enters. Young adult. Nervy. Also wearing white—816123—and clutching a bedroll. CORCORAN looks up.

Beat. MILLET takes in CORCORAN and FILIGREE and the two cots.

MILLET: Oh. Oh, sorry, think I must have got the wrong room.

MILLET turns to exit and stops abruptly as the door shuts in its face. Turns back. Shrugs apologetically.

(Looks like you're stuck with me.)

CORCORAN: New or transfer?

MILLET: Sorry?

CORCORAN: Are you new? Or are you a transfer?

MILLET: Oh. Oh, new. I think. I mean, I *transferred* from the (city)—you know, but not from another (place like this).

Beat.

So I suppose—

CORCORAN: New, then.

MILLET: Yeah. New. Yeah.

Pause.

Where should I . . . ?

CORCORAN: ?

MILLET holds up its bedroll.

Wherever you like.

MILLET: Just there's only two cots, so . . . And there's three of us. So . . .

CORCORAN: Over there, if you like.

MILLET: But then where are you going to sleep?

CORCORAN shrugs, gestures at FILIGREE's cot.

Alright, and then that one sleeps there, I suppose, and we all go round again.

CORCORAN: Filigree.

MILLET: Eh?

CORCORAN: That one. Filigree.

MILLET: I didn't think we got to have names.

CORCORAN: No one can stop you having a name.

MILLET: Right. Right then. Well, I'm Millet.

CORCORAN: There you go.

CORCORAN returns to the crossword. MILLET indicates a chair.

MILLET: Do you mind?

CORCORAN: (Be my guest.)

MILLET sits. Looks around.

MILLET: Here, I was supposed to get a shower, wasn't I?

CORCORAN: In the morning, I should think.

MILLET: Not till the morning?

CORCORAN: Better in the morning. More hot water.

MILLET: Oh. Oh, well, that's nice. Something to look forward to, eh?

Silence.

I suppose it might be a clerical error. Eh? The three of us. Must be a clerical error.

CORCORAN: *(without looking up)* Wouldn't have thought so. I expect one of us is moving on soon, is what it is.

MILLET: Moving on?

CORCORAN: Then there won't be three of us. Only two.

   MILLET *becomes rather small, clutching its bedroll.*

Do you want a carrot?

MILLET: A—?

CORCORAN: Carrot.

MILLET: A *real* carrot?

   CORCORAN *wheels over to the empty cot, rummages under the pillow.*

How've you got a carrot?

CORCORAN: My birthday. Got a bag.

MILLET: A bag?!

CORCORAN: *Small* bag.

   CORCORAN *produces a bag with two carrots in it. Holds one out to* MILLET.

MILLET: You sure?

MILLET goes and takes the carrot. It is an old and squashy carrot.

When was your birthday?

CORCORAN: Give it back then.

MILLET: No, I—

CORCORAN: Go on, give it back.

MILLET: No, sorry, it's lovely. Lovely carrot. Thank you.

MILLET takes the carrot and tucks in. CORCORAN removes the other carrot from the bag, lovingly smells its length, then carefully places it back in the bag, wraps it up, and puts it back under the pillow. MILLET self-consciously stops eating, mid-enthusiastic chew. It starts to eat the carrot with reverence. Eventually stops eating it altogether. Looks for somewhere to store the carrot. The other pillow would seem the right place, but FILIGREE's head is on it. MILLET looks at FILIGREE with growing concern.

Here. Is it . . . ?

CORCORAN: ?

MILLET: It's not moving.

CORCORAN: It's asleep.

MILLET: Are you sure, cos it's not moving.

CORCORAN: Been swimming.

MILLET: *(alarmed)* I can't swim!

CORCORAN: Needs must, and all that.

MILLET: But I can't swim!

CORCORAN: No one said you had to.

MILLET: (shit oh shit oh shit oh shit . . .)

CORCORAN: Hey!
Millet.
Eat your carrot.

> MILLET *disconsolately chews on the carrot.* CORCORAN *returns to the crossword.* FILIGREE's *eyes suddenly open and stare at* MILLET. MILLET *notices and jumps.*

MILLET: Oh, thank God!

(to CORCORAN*)* Here, it's awake!

(to FILIGREE*)* I thought you were—

> *Without warning,* FILIGREE *hurtles at* MILLET *and attacks it.* MILLET *defends itself as best it can. There is a soft "ding!" and the sound of the door opening. A warm automated voice speaks.*

VOICE: 455743 C.

> FILIGREE *gets up and exits. Door closes. Breathless,* MILLET *picks itself up, checks its lip and nose for blood.* CORCORAN *looks up briefly.*

CORCORAN: It's in and out like a bloody yo-yo. "C" did they say?

MILLET: What?

CORCORAN: Blood tests, I should think. Something like that.

CORCORAN returns to the crossword.

MILLET: Sorry, what—what just happened? What just happened there?

CORCORAN: ?

MILLET: Then. The the the *ninja* attack—what's that about?

CORCORAN: I should think Filigree was worried you were going to take its cot.

MILLET: I wasn't anywhere near Filigree's bloody cot. Filigree was on Filigree's cot—I was over here!

CORCORAN shrugs.

CORCORAN: Still.

MILLET: So, what, are we gonna have to fight it out in Thunderdome?

CORCORAN: Shouldn't think so.

CORCORAN thinks. A flicker of concern.

Unless we're asked to, of course. But I don't see what purpose that would serve.

MILLET: I'll just keep myself to myself then. I'll just keep myself to myself.

Pause.

CORCORAN: So it's real then? Thunderdome?

MILLET: What?

CORCORAN: I'd heard rumours.

MILLET: About—?

CORCORAN: Thunder/dome—

MILLET: Thunderdome? What?

CORCORAN: I'd heard rumours.

MILLET: That it's real?

CORCORAN: Is it?

MILLET: Is it?

CORCORAN: I don't know.

MILLET: You brought it up!

CORCORAN: No. You brought it up.

MILLET: I was referencing a film. Like, joking.

CORCORAN: Oh. Well. I'd heard rumours.

MILLET: That Thunderdome is real. That's—

CORCORAN: I know.

MILLET: That's preposterous.

CORCORAN: I know.

MILLET: I mean, what purpose would it serve?

CORCORAN: That's what I said.

MILLET: What would it be for? I mean!

CORCORAN: Entertainment, I suppose.

    Pause.

MILLET: It's not, is it?

CORCORAN: / What?

MILLET: Real?

    CORCORAN shrugs.

Who'd you hear it from?

CORCORAN: Got you worried there.

MILLET: What?

CORCORAN: Got you worried.

MILLET: You're a bastard.

CORCORAN: Oh come on. Be a bit frivolous, wouldn't it?

MILLET: That's not funny.

CORCORAN: Bit funny.

MILLET: Bastard.

MILLET *limps pointedly to* CORCORAN'S *cot and sits.* CORCORAN *looks at* MILLET. MILLET *gets up sharply. Beat.*

Do you mind?

CORCORAN: (Be my guest.)

MILLET *sits on the cot, wincing. Pats it. Bounces a bit. Seems pleased by the buoyancy. Momentarily forgets about its bruises. Smooths the blanket—finds it soft and holds it to its face.*

MILLET: Here, what do you think this is—angora?

CORCORAN: Shouldn't think so.

MILLET: It's nice though, innit.

CORCORAN: Environmental enrichment.

MILLET: Soft. Soft enough to be angora. You don't know—it could be.

CORCORAN: You ever felt angora?

MILLET: I don't know—you ever been to the Flatlands?

CORCORAN: Got angora there, do they?

MILLET: No. I don't know. But—*I've been.* You ever been?

CORCORAN *shakes its head.*

CORCORAN: Never left Hightower.

MILLET: Really? Never? Ooh, you haven't lived.

CORCORAN: Nice is it then, the Flatlands?

MILLET: No. No, well, no, I mean, it's just . . . flat.

CORCORAN: Opposite of Hightower then.

MILLET: Yeah. Yeah, complete opposite of Hightower! Went out there a coupla times when I was younger. My uncle had a place.

CORCORAN: Like a holiday / place?

MILLET: Nothing so grand, no, I wish, I mean—no. He skipped out on the Eye. Knew he wasn't gonna pass so he just *(whistles)* scarpered— you know. He had a little cabin. Mum used to take him things he needed—bit of dried food, stuff like that. Sometimes I'd go with her.

CORCORAN: Nice little holiday.

MILLET: You know, it was. Even just sitting in that grass and smelling the air.

CORCORAN: Grass?

MILLET: Yeah—all kinds. Just growing, just like that.

CORCORAN: Ever see any animals?

MILLET: Not so much.

Beat.

I touched a cow once.

CORCORAN: A cow?

MILLET: Dead cow.

CORCORAN: Doesn't count.

MILLET: Still a cow.

Pause.

So what's wrong with it, then?

CORCORAN: ?

MILLET: (The other one)—what's wrong with it?

CORCORAN: I don't know.

MILLET: You said blood tests, what are they for?

CORCORAN: Maybe blood tests.

MILLET: Yeah, what are they for? Rabies?

CORCORAN: Wouldn't have thought so.

MILLET: I was joking. Cos of (rrraaaarrrrgghhhh). You know? What are they for then, the blood tests?

CORCORAN: Don't know if it is blood tests.

MILLET: You said.

CORCORAN: I was guessing.

MILLET: Oh.

CORCORAN: Could be a lot of things.

MILLET: Like what?

CORCORAN: Suspension study. Not behavioural, probably. Biopsy, maybe.

MILLET: What for?

CORCORAN: What?

MILLET: Biopsy.

CORCORAN: I don't know. Don't know if it is a biopsy.

MILLET: You said.

CORCORAN: I was guessing.

MILLET: Oh.

   Beat.

How do you know so much about it?

CORCORAN: I'm a scientist.

   Beat.

MILLET: *(small laugh)* Alright, fair enough. I'd like to know what's wrong with it, that's all.

CORCORAN: This isn't a hospital, you know. It isn't a care facility.

MILLET: I know. It's just there's something wrong with it.

MILLET taps its head.

It's not normal.

CORCORAN: You're basing that on very short acquaintance.

Pause.

MILLET: He's dead now, of course. My uncle.

CORCORAN: Did he get got?

MILLET nods.

MILLET: Hardly worth it really, was it? Running off, all that trouble.

CORCORAN: I dunno. Few years of air and grass—I wouldn't say no.

MILLET: I'd have loved to have been a farmer. Must've been a nice job, eh? I could've done that. I'd be a good farmer. I mean, doesn't take a genius, does it? In fact, you don't want geniuses, do you? Farming? That'd be silly, wouldn't it?

CORCORAN: Was that what your uncle did then? Farming?

MILLET: In the Flatlands? Can't farm in the Flatlands.

CORCORAN: (Fair point.)

Pause.

I had a bit of lunch the other day, could've sworn it was cardboard dipped in lard. No, no, I'm not—I think that's really what it was.

MILLET: See? Farming. That's the ticket.

Beat.

Where are you from?

CORCORAN: South.

MILLET: Oh, yeah? Actually, yeah, now you mention it, I might have guessed that. You've got a sort of look.

CORCORAN looks up, quizzical.

Not a look. Dunno why I said look. Accent. I meant accent.

CORCORAN: I don't think I do.

MILLET: No. No, you don't. I dunno why I said that. Dunno what a southern "look" would be, either.

Pause.

We always do that, don't we? Eh? You say you're from, I dunno, New Bridgeford, and I say, oh yeah, I know where New Bridgeford is, my cousin lives in New Bridgeford, everyone from New Bridgeford sounds like you, or looks like you, or's got webbed toes, or whatever, and then we've got a reason to chat, right—even though I've never heard of where you're from, I don't know nothing about it, and you wouldn't care, not really, but we're really shit at just talking. We're really shit at it.

Beat. CORCORAN *returns to the crossword.*

I think we *used* to be good at it. Before.

CORCORAN: Doesn't matter what you say in here.

MILLET: I think it does. We can all strive to raise the bar.

Pause.

CORCORAN: "Small dog or cat, perhaps—it has energy."

MILLET: What?

CORCORAN: Ten across. "Small dog or cat, perhaps—it has energy."

CORCORAN looks up hopefully. MILLET looks blank.

MILLET: What is that, a cryptic? I don't do cryptics.

CORCORAN goes back to the crossword.

Hey, that doesn't mean anything!

CORCORAN: I know.

MILLET: I'm not stupid!

Pause.

Ever heard of the Fibonacci sequence?

CORCORAN: Eh?

MILLET: Do you know what the Fibonacci sequence is? It's numbers, but numbers in a list, so you add the number to the number before it to get the next number. I can do it up to, like, in the thousands. My dad taught me. Do you want to see me do it?

Beat.

CORCORAN: Go on then.

MILLET: Right. One. One. Two. Three. Five. Eight. Thirteen. Twenty-one. Thirty-four. Fifty-five. Eighty-nine . . .

Pauses for addition.

One hundred and / forty-four—

CORCORAN: Why's there two ones?

MILLET: What?

CORCORAN: Why's there two / ones?

MILLET: Why are you—you interrupted me.

CORCORAN: Sorry.

MILLET: I was on a roll.

CORCORAN: Sorry.

MILLET: What do you mean, why's there two ones?

CORCORAN: At the beginning. You said one one.

MILLET: To make two. One and one makes two.

CORCORAN: How do you get to start with two ones?

MILLET: What? I don't know. Otherwise you couldn't add it to anything. You'd just have one.

CORCORAN: Yeah.

MILLET: It wouldn't be a sequence, it would just be "one."

CORCORAN: It would, yeah.

MILLET: But that—okay, the one has been cloned, alright? There's a one and a clone one and you put them together and get two. Make sense?

Pause. The hiss of the door and a soft "ding."

VOICE: 622149 C.

MILLET again checks its number, but CORCORAN wheels towards the door. Pauses.

CORCORAN: "C," did they say?

MILLET nods. CORCORAN grunts and exits. MILLET paces, looking around. Finds a deck of cards, begins to shuffle them, and attempts a trick. The shuffling becomes more and more ambitious until MILLET accidentally sprays the deck everywhere.

MILLET: Shit.

MILLET remembers the security camera.

(Shit.)

MILLET self-consciously clears up the cards. Thinks.

One, one, two—*zero*, one one! That's it, it's cos it starts with nothing, that it's, yeah, zero—zero, one, one. Okay, lemme try again. Okay. *Zero*, one, one, two, three, five, eight, thirteen, twenty-one, thirty-four, fifty-five, eighty-nine, one hundred and forty-four, two—two hundred and . . . thirty-three, three hundred and seventy-seven, (four, five, seventy, eighty, plus . . .) six hundred and ten . . . nine hundred and eighty-seven . . . one thousand and . . .

Lights fade over MILLET*'s recitation. A beauty product commercial plays, e.g., Olay.*

*Lights up—*MILLET *is asleep on the floor, having taken a blanket and pillow from one of the cots.* FILIGREE *is crouched over it.* MILLET *wakes up, starts, and then tries to lie as still as possible.*

FILIGREE: I thought you were dead.

MILLET: Nope. Nope, not dead.

FILIGREE: Why are you on the floor?

MILLET: Didn't think I should take a cot.

FILIGREE: Why not?

Beat.

MILLET: No reason.

FILIGREE: That's what they're there for. Sleeping on.

FILIGREE *stares for a moment, then pats* MILLET *on the head, goes over to its cot, and starts sketching on a pad.* MILLET *watches cautiously.*

Beat.

MILLET: Has there been breakfast, do you know?

FILIGREE: *(shrugs)* I just got back.

MILLET: You were gone all night?

FILIGREE: Suppose so.

MILLET: Would I'd known.

> MILLET *gets up and scratches, giving* FILIGREE *a wide berth,*
> *but* FILIGREE *is intent on its pad.* MILLET *picks up the sheet*
> *and pillow from the floor to return them to the cot. Spots the*
> *carrot bag.*

Here, you don't think we *missed* breakfast, do you?

FILIGREE: Maybe.

MILLET: What, really?

FILIGREE: It's never very nice.

MILLET: Still. I'm starving.

> MILLET *looks longingly at the carrot bag.*

Where's the other one?

FILIGREE: Corcoran.

MILLET: Corco/ran?

FILIGREE: Corcoran.

MILLET: Corcoran, bloody hell, that's a set of shoes to fill. Where's Corcoran?

FILIGREE shrugs.

Do you think it's coming back?

FILIGREE: *(sharply)* Yes.

MILLET: Alright, alright!

MILLET replaces the pillow on top of the carrot, smooths it. FILIGREE returns to its drawing. MILLET paces about a bit, steering clear of FILIGREE. FILIGREE suddenly wiggles violently, enthusiastically rubbing its back against the bed. MILLET jumps. FILIGREE instantly returns to calm stillness. MILLET watches.

What are you doing there?

FILIGREE: Drawing.

MILLET: What are you drawing?

FILIGREE: You.

MILLET: Can I see?

FILIGREE looks up steadily.

FILIGREE: If you really want to.

Beat.

MILLET: That's alright.

> FILIGREE *returns to the pad.* MILLET *paces. Stretches. Catches a whiff of its own armpit.*

(Bloody hell!) God! I'm festering! I was supposed to get a shower this morning. Oh, I hope I didn't sleep through the call—I'm bloody festering. Tell you what, it's you and whatsit, Corcoran, I feel sorry for. You can probably smell me from over there!

FILIGREE: Yeah.

MILLET: What, can you really?

> FILIGREE *looks up, nods sadly.*

Sorry. Do you want me to—? I could—

> MILLET *moves as far away from* FILIGREE *as it can.*

That better?

> FILIGREE *slowly shakes its head, and then watches as* MILLET *backs away another step, and then another, until it is crammed into a corner.*

> FILIGREE *returns to its drawing.* MILLET *stands in the corner. Looks around from its position. Unthinking it takes a step forward.* FILIGREE's *head snaps round and* MILLET *shoots back into the corner, eyeballing* FILIGREE.

> *The hiss of the door opening.* CORCORAN *enters. Looks from one to the other.* FILIGREE *looks guilty.*

CORCORAN: We talked about this sort of thing.

(to MILLET) Take a seat, for Christ's sake—it's not going to do anything.

MILLET: Easy for you to say.

CORCORAN: Did you apologize?

FILIGREE: For what?

CORCORAN: Did you apologize?

FILIGREE: It's humiliating.

CORCORAN: No, it's what we do. Poor Millet's going to stay in the corner till you do.

FILIGREE shrugs.

CORCORAN stares.

FILIGREE sighs.

FILIGREE: *(parroting)* I have no parents, and apparently a childhood and ensuing maturation with no maternal or paternal influence or affection of any kind has "critically impacted my ability to socialize normally."

MILLET: No shit.

CORCORAN: And?

FILIGREE: What?

CORCORAN: "I'm very sorry."

FILIGREE: I already apologized.

CORCORAN: No, you / didn't—

MILLET: It's alright.

FILIGREE: I explained.

CORCORAN: It's not the same thing.

MILLET: It's alright, / really.

CORCORAN: No, it's not. I'm very / sorry.

MILLET: It's / alright!

CORCORAN: *I'm very sorry.*

    Beat.

FILIGREE: I'm very sorry.

MILLET: It's alright.

    MILLET doesn't move.

CORCORAN: Stop quivering in the bloody corner—you'll only encourage it.

    MILLET comes out of the corner cautiously. CORCORAN retrieves its newspaper and resumes the crossword.

MILLET: Where were you?

CORCORAN: (Don't know.) I was asleep. Did you get your shower yet?

MILLET: (No.) Haven't even had breakfast.

CORCORAN: You'll get your shower first, I'd think. Before breakfast.

MILLET: Before breakfast, is it?

CORCORAN: I'd've thought so.

MILLET: . . . bloody starving . . .

Silence. FILIGREE *suddenly rubs its back again. Stillness.*

Thank you.

CORCORAN: Eh?

MILLET: Thank you. You know. For . . .

CORCORAN: Just manners, isn't it.

MILLET: Yeah, but. Look, can I have a word?

CORCORAN: Yes.

MILLET: Just—over here.

MILLET *wheels* CORCORAN *a little away from* FILIGREE, *who seems oblivious.*

Look, do you think there's any way I could, you know, not be alone with it again?

CORCORAN: What are you asking *me* for?

MILLET: I don't know, couldn't you—ask?

CORCORAN: You ask.

MILLET: Or have a word with it.

CORCORAN: Just did.

MILLET: No, you know, I mean, saying sorry's fine, but it could've ripped my bloody throat out last night.

CORCORAN: Oh, now . . .

MILLET: It could!

CORCORAN: I doubt it.

MILLET: What if it does it again? Sorry's not much good then, is it?

CORCORAN: It doesn't get violent.

MILLET: It doesn't—? What was that, then?

CORCORAN: Atavism, most like.

MILLET: Ata—whatever.

CORCORAN: An atavistic response to competition for resources.

MILLET: Yeah, okay, look, whatever, what if it does it again when you're not here?

FILIGREE: I won't.

MILLET: Eh?

FILIGREE: I was just surprised to see you.

CORCORAN: Winding it up, more like.

FILIGREE: I promise I won't do it again.

MILLET: You heard all that?

CORCORAN: It's got really good hearing.

MILLET: Why didn't you tell me?

CORCORAN: Didn't know you was telling secrets.

MILLET: Not secrets—not *secrets*—just private.

FILIGREE: You want to talk in private, you'll have to go next door.

MILLET: What's next door?

FILIGREE: Don't know. Never been.

MILLET: But you can go next door?

FILIGREE: Shouldn't think so.

MILLET: You're an obstructive little bugger, aren't you?

>FILIGREE *makes a sudden movement towards* MILLET, *who scampers back.*

CORCORAN: Oh, stop reacting to it, for Pete's sake. It's not going to do anything.

FILIGREE: I might.

CORCORAN: No. You won't.

>*Beat.*

FILIGREE: There's this theory, you know. That the baseline function of the brain, if you take away parental nurturing and moral conditioning and social education and blah de blah, that the brain's purest core imperative is murder.

Beat.

MILLET: Lovely.

MILLET mouths "not normal!" at CORCORAN. FILIGREE makes another sudden movement. MILLET scampers back again.

FILIGREE grins and continues sketching. MILLET makes another gesture to CORCORAN, who dismisses it and returns to the crossword. MILLET putters about, bored and tense.

MILLET examines its environment much as an unpanicked caged animal might. Notices an air vent, climbs up to it, peers through.

Hey! Here, you'll never guess what—there *is* a next door and all! Hello? Here, come and have a look.

CORCORAN looks up from its seat in its wheelchair. An embarrassed beat.

There's three more over there. Helloooo! Hellooooooooo! Nah, can't hear me. Hellllooooooooooo!!!!

MILLET rattles the air vent.

Hellooooooooooo! Here, you know, if I could get this thing off . . .

CORCORAN: No, no, don't do that.

MILLET: But I bet I could talk to them if I could get—

CORCORAN: You'll make a mess. Then someone'll have to come in and fix it.

MILLET stops sharply. A "ding" and the door opens—MILLET jumps.

VOICE: 816123 A.

Beat.

CORCORAN: That'll be you, then.

MILLET: Eh?

CORCORAN: That'll be you. Your shower.

MILLET: Right. Right! Lovely. See you in a bit then.

MILLET exits. CORCORAN looks at the air vent. Wheels over and cocks its head to listen. FILIGREE gets up, goes and peers through the air vent. Turns to CORCORAN.

FILIGREE: Why's there three? Over there. Three here, three there. There's always just two.

CORCORAN: That's what I thought.

Beat.

LD50, I should think.

FILIGREE: LD50?

CORCORAN: Best not.

FILIGREE returns to its cot and its drawing.

Not likely to be you anyway, my love. You've got too much still to give.

FILIGREE rubs its back violently again. CORCORAN scratches its eye and winces, repeats the scratching. FILIGREE draws and CORCORAN does its crossword.

Lights down.

A cleaning or beauty product commercial—e.g., Lysol. Lights up.

CORCORAN and FILIGREE are as before. MILLET is now back sitting cross-legged on CORCORAN's cot.

MILLET: —bloody nice soap, it was. Lovely, all, like fat whatsit, lather. Nice smell, too. I haven't had soap like that, since, well—I wonder what it is, eh? What makes a nice fat lather like that?

CORCORAN: Fat, I should think.

MILLET: Could be, could be you're right. Oh, bloody lovely that was, and steaming, you know—you were right, wait for the morning, you said, lots of lovely hot water—oh, I could've stayed in there for hours, I really could. That soap—here, feel my skin.

CORCORAN: You're alright.

FILIGREE: I want to.

MILLET: It's nothing special.

FILIGREE: Come on. I want to feel it. Bring me your skin.

MILLET approaches reluctantly. FILIGREE strokes its arm, then runs its cheek along it. Then bites it.

MILLET: OW! What the— What are you doing?

FILIGREE blinks innocently.

CORCORAN: What did it do?

MILLET: Bit me!

FILIGREE: Is that not allowed?

MILLET: / No!

CORCORAN: Really trying it on, you are.

MILLET: No, it's not allowed! You stay away from me.

FILIGREE: I did. You came over here.

MILLET: Yeah! But you! Just don't, alright? Just—bloody . . . ow . . .

MILLET retires dismally to the cot. CORCORAN glares at FILIGREE.

CORCORAN: Be nice.

FILIGREE scratches its back again.

MILLET: Be nice? Thanks for stepping in. Bloody—

FILIGREE: I was just joking.

MILLET: You bit me.

FILIGREE: Just trying to make friends.

MILLET: You bit me.

FILIGREE: I have no parents, and going through / childhood and subsequent—

MILLET: Yeah, yeah. That's why you didn't make it through the Eye, cos you're a bloody psychopath.

CORCORAN: / Hey!

FILIGREE: What did you say?

MILLET: You heard. You're a bloody psychopath.

FILIGREE: That's a horrible thing to say.

MILLET: You bit me!

FILIGREE: That's a horrible thing to say! I / could've—

MILLET: Yeah, well, you're pretty bloody / horrible.

CORCORAN: / Alright—

FILIGREE: I could've passed it—you / don't know!

MILLET: Horrible bloody / psychopath—

CORCORAN: / Hey!

FILIGREE: You don't know, I could've passed it if they'd let me / take it—

MILLET: If they'd / let you?

FILIGREE: I could've passed it if they'd let me / take it!

MILLET: And why didn't they let you, eh? Because you're a *bloody psychopath!*

> *FILIGREE roars and launches at MILLET, who avoids the attack— they scamper around the room.*

CORCORAN: Alright. Alright! Stop now. Stop it! STOP! IT!

> *MILLET makes a last futile bat at FILIGREE. FILIGREE, however, has already become completely distracted by scratching its back.*

Here, what's going on there?

FILIGREE: Don't know. It's really itchy.

> *FILIGREE turns, like a dog chasing its tail, trying to work out what's going on with its back. CORCORAN tries to catch it and hold it still.*

CORCORAN: Hold on, hold on, here, come here. That's it. Alright, let's have a look.

> *CORCORAN lifts FILIGREE's shirt to reveal a large gauze pad.*

You've got something stuck to you. Let's have a look.

> *CORCORAN peels back the pad to reveal a large suture wound.*

FILIGREE: What is it?

CORCORAN: Kidney, I'd say.

FILIGREE: Added or missing?

CORCORAN: How many did you have before?

FILIGREE shrugs.

CORCORAN gently palpates FILIGREE's back.

... hard to tell ...

MILLET: Can I try?

CORCORAN: What, are you a doctor now?

MILLET: No. But ...

MILLET shrugs.

CORCORAN: Thought they said "C." That's a "D" procedure.

FILIGREE: What is?

CORCORAN: "D" procedure, something like that. Shouldn't give you a "C" call if it's gonna be—you oughta get some bloody warning.

MILLET: Can I see?

MILLET comes and peers closely at the wound over CORCORAN's shoulder.

CORCORAN: Does it hurt?

FILIGREE: Just itches.

MILLET reaches out and touches the skin surrounding the wound—CORCORAN slaps its hand away.

Hey!

MILLET: I wasn't, I wasn't!

FILIGREE: Don't!

CORCORAN: You watch it—you'll get your hands trimmed.

MILLET: I wasn't!

MILLET moves away as CORCORAN replaces the pad.

Sensitive . . .

CORCORAN: Just try not to scratch at it—you'll pull out the stitches.

FILIGREE: But it's itchy.

MILLET: Alright if it bites *me* . . .

MILLET disconsolately returns to peering through the air vent.

CORCORAN: Do your drawings. That'll take your mind off it.

FILIGREE: I've finished.

CORCORAN: Let's have a look then.

MILLET: Wouldn't let me look.

FILIGREE: Yes I did—you didn't want to.

MILLET: Because you were weird about it.

FILIGREE: Do you want to then?

MILLET: No.

CORCORAN: Come on then.

    CORCORAN looks at the sketch, grunts in laughter.

FILIGREE: You like it.

CORCORAN: Who is it? Is it—?

FILIGREE: *That* one! (Obviously!)

CORCORAN: Millet? Right, yeah, alright, I can see that. All the . . . yeah, okay. That's Millet.

MILLET: It's me?

CORCORAN: Alright, try and do another one—

FILIGREE: You don't like it.

CORCORAN: Well, it's—

MILLET: I want to see it.

CORCORAN: No you don't.

FILIGREE: But you laughed.

CORCORAN: I did, yeah. But—

MILLET: What, did it draw me really fat or something?

CORCORAN: No.

MILLET: Come on, I want to see.

CORCORAN: No. You don't.

MILLET: *(to FILIGREE)* You're horrible, you are. You're really horrible.

CORCORAN: Alright—just . . .

> MILLET *grumpily goes back to the air vent.*

Try and do another one.

FILIGREE: Of what—of that one?

CORCORAN: Of Millet, yeah. And this time, remember what you say. Remember what you say?

FILIGREE: Kindness is my friend.

CORCORAN: That's right, kindness is your friend. So you do another picture of Millet, and think about how kindess / is your friend.

FILIGREE: Kindness is my friend.

CORCORAN: That's right. Alright?

> FILIGREE *thinks, nods, and then kisses* CORCORAN *hard on the head.*

MILLET: Here, they've got breakfast! They've got breakfast over there! Nice bowls. Green. Nice colour, green. Nice, that. Bit of colour in our lives, eh?

CORCORAN: It'll be on its way, then. Only a matter of time.

MILLET: I hope so—my stomach's starting to digest itself.

There is a soft "ding." A tray with two bowls appear—they are green and bear the designations 622149 A and 455743 B.

What? Oh, come on—have we got to share or something?

Another "ding."

VOICE: Commencing LD50.

Another green bowl appears—816123 E.

MILLET: Okay, there we go, thank you very much.

CORCORAN: Here, don't just grab anything—your number's on your bowl.

MILLET: I know, I know—look.

MILLET points to its number and then the bowl.

See?

CORCORAN looks at the bowl.

CORCORAN: Yeah, no, I'll have that one.

MILLET: What, no. / No, you said—

CORCORAN: Yep, I'll have / that one—

MILLET: You said don't just grab / anything—

CORCORAN: Just give / me it and—

MILLET: Don't just grab anything, you said. / Well, this one's got my number—

CORCORAN: Seriously, just give / it me. Please.

MILLET: This one's got my number / and I'm having it.

CORCORAN: Please.

MILLET: Look, there's yours. There.

CORCORAN: I think they got us mixed up.

MILLET: This one's got my number and I'm having it.

CORCORAN: I just think they got us mixed up.

MILLET: Right, right.

> MILLET *settles down on the cot and tucks in with relish.*
> *Immediately spits it out.*

Bloody Nora—you weren't wrong, this tastes like drain cleaner!

FILIGREE: Told you.

MILLET: You haven't got a line on any more of those carrots, have you?

FILIGREE: Better eat it. Or you'll get the tube.

MILLET: You know, I'm that bloody hungry . . .

MILLET swallows another mouthful and grimaces.

You're not having a problem.

FILIGREE: Used to it.

MILLET: Yeah yeah, probably your insides are made out of, like, concrete.

FILIGREE: And yours are made out of old poo.

MILLET: Out of / old—

FILIGREE: Old poo. Soft old poo.

MILLET: You're just—

CORCORAN: Can it.

MILLET: No, seriously. That's just—

CORCORAN: Can it.

MILLET: . . . I haven't done anything.

They continue to eat in silence. FILIGREE finishes its food and licks the bowl. The licking becomes more enthusiastic until it is actually chewing the sides.

CORCORAN: You'll break your teeth.

FILIGREE pauses for a second, gazing at CORCORAN, big puppy eyes over the bowl's edge. Then continues with a deliberate vengeance.

Filigree.

FILIGREE stops.

MILLET: Nothing to read in here, eh?

CORCORAN: You can have this when I'm done.

MILLET: How old's that?

CORCORAN, with thought, turns the newspaper over, looks for the date, and starts to work out how old it is.

(continuous) Yeah, no, sorry, I mean, I appreciate it, but I mean, when did they stop making those? Eh? Must be, you know, anyway that's probably all just old . . . election results or something. Like a book. You ever read a book?

CORCORAN: Yes, I've read a book.

MILLET: Well, sorry, I mean, you never know, do you.

CORCORAN: Seventeen years.

MILLET: Eh?

CORCORAN: That's how old this is. Seventeen years. Not in bad nick, is it?

MILLET: Yeah. No, it's . . . really nice. Lovely.

CORCORAN grunts appreciatively.

What's your favourite book then? Unless, well, you've read more than one / book, right?

CORCORAN: Yes, I've read more than one / book.

MILLET: Alright, sorry, you never know, do you. What's your favourite book, then?

CORCORAN thinks.

I know, it's difficult, isn't it? Tell you what mine is? *Finnegans Wake.*

CORCORAN: Joyce?

CORCORAN grunts mild approval.

MILLET: Read it?

CORCORAN: Couldn't get through it.

MILLET: Oh, it's my favourite, *Finnegans Wake.* Brilliant.

CORCORAN: Couldn't get through it.

MILLET: Brilliant.

FILIGREE: What's it about?

MILLET: It's not about what, it's about how. You know, the style, language and stuff. Brilliant.

FILIGREE: But what's the story?

MILLET: It's, well, it's, it's hard to—how would you describe *Finnegans Wake*?

CORCORAN: I wouldn't. I couldn't get through it.

MILLET: Alright, well, basically, it's about, like, this character called Finnegan. And he dies, right, and then everyone comes to his funeral.

FILIGREE: And?

MILLET: And that's it. Well, there's more to it, like, character stuff. All the people that come to the funeral.

CORCORAN has a very very tiny smile.

What?

CORCORAN shakes head, "nothing."

CORCORAN: Sounds about right.

MILLET: No books at all.

CORCORAN: You can have this when I'm done if you like.

MILLET: What happened to environmental enrichment? Eh?

FILIGREE: That sounds like a lousy story.

MILLET: What?

FILIGREE: *That* does. I wouldn't want to read that story.

MILLET: No, well, like I said—

FILIGREE: Corcoran's stories are best.

MILLET: Oh, yeah? Bit of a storyteller, are you?

FILIGREE: Corcoran has the best stories.

MILLET: Let's have one then.

CORCORAN: Doing the crossword, aren't I?

MILLET: Crossword's been there for seventeen years, apparently. Come on! Let's have a story!

CORCORAN: *(to FILIGREE)* You're a bloody pain, you are. Alright. What sort of story do you want?

FILIGREE: *(there is ritual to this)* Corcoran oh Corcoran—why do you sit in that chair?

CORCORAN: Alright. Let's see. Alright. When I was a small child, about five years old, I decided that I wanted to be . . .

FILIGREE: A ballet dancer.

CORCORAN: A ballet dancer? Alright, a ballet dancer. (Bloody hell, ballet dancer.) Alright, I decided I wanted to be a ballet dancer. So I danced around the house all day—I had to practise, you see.

FILIGREE: Did you know how to be a ballet dancer already?

CORCORAN: No. But I thought if I tried hard enough, and danced until my feet were sore and broken, I thought I'd learn. I thought I'd get to be so good at being a ballet dancer that one day I'd be named Grand High Magical Toes of the Perfect Pointe at the Hightower Ballet Corps.

MILLET: That really what it's called?

CORCORAN shrugs—I don't know.

CORCORAN: Yeah. And you know what the Grand High Magical Toes of the Perfect Pointe gets to do? Not just dance the leading dance at the annual celebration of the Eye, and get a beautiful place to live in the highest of all the towers in Hightower, and get cake on your birthday, but, best of all, you get a special pair of wings.

FILIGREE: What are they for?

CORCORAN: Well, they're very special indeed. Only the Grand High Magical Toes gets to wear them. I thought if I could get those wings, I could leap from the top of the highest tower in Hightower and dance among the clouds. So off I went, straight to the headquarters of the Hightower Ballet Corps, and asked if they would teach me.

Teach you? they said. But you don't even have the proper shoes! So off I went, disheartened and sure I was never gonna be a ballet dancer after all, cos where was I gonna get the proper shoes? And then, sitting right there in front of me, was a very, very old person, all wrinkly and thin, with its shabby feet jammed into the perfectest pair of ballet shoes you ever did see. I'm ever so hungry, it said, could you give me something to eat? If you give me something to eat, I'll give you these shoes right off my feet.

FILIGREE: It was a ballet dancer that talked in rhymes!

CORCORAN: Just at that moment it was.

FILIGREE: A poem-talking ballet dancer.

CORCORAN: Well, no, not all the time, no, it made that rhyme by accident—nothing else it said rhymed.

MILLET: Sure? Sounds to me like the kind of character that talks in poems.

CORCORAN: I was there, wasn't I?

FILIGREE: Poems.

CORCORAN: No poems. So, it just happened that I always carried a bit of bread in my satchel. A bit of bread and some—dried peas, just in case I got lost, right? But right then the only thing that was important was getting some proper ballet shoes. So I hand over my little stash, and the old old person gives me the shoes, and off I run, right back to the Ballet Corps, and ask if they'll teach me now that I have shoes. Teach you? they said. But you don't even have the proper outfit! So away I went, sure I was never gonna be a ballet dancer now—cos where was I going to get the proper outfit? I wandered and wandered, feeling ever so sad, till I found myself in an enchanted forest.

MILLET: An—?

CORCORAN: Enchanted forest.

MILLET: An enchanted forest.

CORCORAN: Yeah.

MILLET: Alright.

CORCORAN: And right there, in the / enchanted forest—

FILIGREE: Why was it enchanted?

CORCORAN: Eh?

FILIGREE: Why was / it enchanted?

CORCORAN: I don't know—cos a sorcerer put a spell on it.

FILIGREE: What's a sorcerer?

CORCORAN: A person that does magic.

FILIGREE: Corcoran oh Corcoran, can I be a sorcerer?

CORCORAN: No. So / there I was—

MILLET: Can I be a sorcerer?

CORCORAN: Just . . .

FILIGREE: Why can't I be / a sorcerer?

CORCORAN: Because you have to learn from when you're a baby. Or best of all you have to get enchanted before you're even born by another sorcerer.

FILIGREE: So who was the first ever sorcerer in the world?

CORCORAN: No one knows. So there I was, in the enchanted forest, when all of a sudden—

FILIGREE: You met the sorcerer.

CORCORAN: No.

FILIGREE: Please / say you met—

CORCORAN: No, he was dead. Killed in a fiery avalanche. *(off* FILIGREE's *raptured expression)* Ah, shit.

FILIGREE: *What's that*?!

CORCORAN: Tomorrow, alright? No, Filigree, tomorrow.

MILLET: So there you were in the enchanted forest . . .

CORCORAN: . . . and right there in front of me was the biggest snake you ever saw. Help me, it said, I'm stuck. I'm stuck in my skin. I need to grow ten times bigger, but I'm stuck in my skin. So I grabbed a hold of its tail and I pulled and I pulled and boom! Out the giant snake popped and swelled to ten times its size.

FILIGREE: And it ate you up.

CORCORAN: . . .

FILIGREE: Why didn't it eat you up?

CORCORAN: Because I helped it get out of its skin. It didn't hurt me, cos it remembered that I was kind to it.

FILIGREE looks perplexed.

MILLET: Psychopath.

CORCORAN: Oi! Thank you for helping me, the snake said, how can I repay you? And I said that all I really wanted was to be the Grand High Magical Toes and get my special wings so I could dance among the clouds. So the snake said here, I'll make you the best ballet dancer outfit that ever there was out of my skin you're holding there in your hands.

MILLET: It was a giant snake that could sew.

CORCORAN: It was a magical (fuc)kin' enchanted snake. Alright? So, good as its word, the snake made me an outfit right out of its skin, and moments later, there I stood, swathed in scales of all blue and green-ish hues, and surely the clothes of the greatest ballet dancer that ever there was. So I ran right back to the Ballet Corps, and ask if they'll teach me, since I now have the proper shoes *and* the proper outfit. Teach you? they said. But do you know how to do the Pirouette of Spectacular Perfection? We can't teach you unless you already know how to do the Pirouette of Spectacular Perfection.

So off I went again, and instead of getting sad and dejected, I taught myself how to do the Pirouette of Spectacular Perfection. It wasn't any good at first, of course, but I practised and practised, everywhere I practised, at home, in the street, by fountains, on treetops, at sunny daybreak, at snowy midnight, on crowded tabletops to the crash of drums, and all alone in the tiny silence of the dark of the belly of a whale. Finally, I found myself on the top of the highest building in all of Hightower, and, there, I finally performed the Pirouette of Spectacular Perfection. Oh, I never felt so happy in all my life. I ran all the way down, through the streets, fast as I could to the Hightower Ballet Corps so I could get the special wings of the Grand High Magical Toes and dance among the clouds. On the way, I was hit by a bus.

Beat. Then FILIGREE *laughs.* MILLET *looks utterly nonplussed.*

Lucky to be alive, really.

VOICE: 455743 B.

FILIGREE gets up and hugs CORCORAN *awkwardly but enthusiastically.*

FILIGREE: Poor Corcoran!

FILIGREE exits.

MILLET: That was a terrible story.

CORCORAN: Thought I did alright.

MILLET: That is the worst story I ever heard.

CORCORAN: Thought I did alright. Filigree liked it.

MILLET: Not really a ringing endorsement, though, is it, Filigree liking something.

CORCORAN delivers a level stare.

What?

CORCORAN returns to the crossword.

Filigree probably likes, you know, watching, you know, cats killing birds, or something.

Beat.

Horrible things, you know. That's what Filigree likes, I bet.

Pause.

CORCORAN: Chew honeydew fruit.

MILLET: What?

CORCORAN fills in the clue.

You've got to give me a chance to think. If you're going to ask.

CORCORAN: Thinking aloud. Sorry.

Pause. CORCORAN peruses the clues. MILLET leans back against the wall, getting dozy.

Don't fall asleep.

MILLET: Eh?

CORCORAN: Don't fall asleep. It'll make your nights very long if you fall asleep now.

MILLET gets up, fractious. Climbs up to look through the vent.

MILLET: Still three of them. Over there, still three of them.

MILLET continues to stare.

They're not doing anything. One of them's got no hands.

CORCORAN: Probably violent.

Beat. MILLET tucks its hands into its armpits.

"Very sad unfinished story about rising smoke."

CORCORAN looks up at MILLET. MILLET continues to stare through the vent. CORCORAN returns to the crossword.

MILLET: Here, why's it got no parents? Filigree. Why's it got no parents?

CORCORAN: Born here.

MILLET: Purpose-bred? Really! What's wrong with it, then?

CORCORAN: ?

MILLET: No, I mean, what was it bred for?

CORCORAN: Study, I suppose.

MILLET: I'll bet it's a knockout model. Eh? Don't you think? I'll bet it is. I wonder what gene they knocked out. Do you know? I've always wanted to meet one. I mean, it's just weird, isn't it?

Pause.

That's why it never went through the Eye then.

CORCORAN: (Probably right.)

MILLET: Well, that's a shame. You know? It should've had the chance. I mean, it might be really clever. Might be really brilliant at, you know, I don't know, gymnastics, or—yeah! Painting, right?

MILLET has gone to pick up FILIGREE's sketch pad.

CORCORAN: Leave that.

MILLET does.

MILLET: Mind you, given the choice, I wouldn't do it again. Stressful, wasn't it? Eh? Do you know, they said it had tightened up just before I took it? Like a week before, they made it way harder.

CORCORAN: That right.

MILLET: Yeah, think about it—if I'd been born a week earlier, if I'd been, like, a week older, I might have passed it. Probably I would've done.

CORCORAN: You're more use in here.

MILLET: I know, betterment of them out there, all that—

CORCORAN: Brighter Family / For a Fitter Future—

MILLET: —For a Fitter Future, yeah, and I support that. I do. Just didn't want to disappoint my mum. You know. She speaks four languages.

CORCORAN: Four?

MILLET: I do too.

CORCORAN: Four?

MILLET: Yeah. No. I mean, I'm bilingual.

CORCORAN: So two.

MILLET: Yeah. I could've learned more.

CORCORAN: What do you speak?

MILLET: French.

CORCORAN: French?

MILLET: Yeah. Oui. Do you speak any other languages?

CORCORAN: (No.)

Beat.

MILLET: Do you want me to do a bit?

Beat.

CORCORAN: Go on then.

MILLET: Alright. "Est ce qu'il y a . . . une . . . pomme de terre?"

Beat.

CORCORAN: Brilliant.

MILLET: / Thanks.

CORCORAN: Brilliant, that is.

MILLET: Thanks. It's from a poem.

CORCORAN: Is it?

MILLET: Yeah.

CORCORAN: Brilliant.

Beat.

"Is there a potato?"

MILLET: What?

CORCORAN: What?

MILLET: You said you didn't speak French!

CORCORAN: I don't.

MILLET: You should've—

CORCORAN: I just know a few words.

MILLET: You should've said.

CORCORAN: Like "potato."

MILLET: I can do loads more than that, you know.

CORCORAN: Yeah—

MILLET: I know loads more words than that.

CORCORAN: Yeah, I'm sure you do.

MILLET: Loads more.

CORCORAN: I'm just teasing.

MILLET: Do you want me to do / a bit more?

CORCORAN: No, it's alright.

MILLET: I'll do some more. I know / loads more.

CORCORAN: No, it's alright, I believe you. I was just teasing.

MILLET: Loads more.

CORCORAN: I believe you. I was just teasing.

Beat.

MILLET: Well, don't.

CORCORAN: Sorry.

Beat.

"Very sad unfinished story about rising smoke."

CORCORAN looks up hopefully. MILLET thinks. Hard. Almost a parody of thinking. Eventually wanders off and looks through the air vent again. CORCORAN returns to the crossword. MILLET suddenly brightens.

MILLET: Here, do you want to see me do a headstand?

Beat.

CORCORAN: Go on then.

MILLET attempts a headstand. Lights fade.

A product commercial, e.g., Axe body spray. Lights rise.

CORCORAN is dozing in its chair. MILLET is fractious, vaguely picking at the furniture. Rubs its eye. Then rubs both.

Gets up, peers through the air vent for a bit. Sits back down again. Picks.

MILLET: You know, I think fish are really underrated.

At the sound of MILLET's voice, CORCORAN starts awake.

I mean, if you take a really big evolutionary step back, we're all fish. We all came from fish. Right. Cos we / evolved from therapsid—

CORCORAN: What time is it?

MILLET looks at its empty wrist.

MILLET: Oh. (Forgot I don't have a watch anymore.)

CORCORAN: (Right.)

CORCORAN looks at FILIGREE's cot, concerned. MILLET watches it. Rubs its eye. Pause.

MILLET: Do you want to play Monopoly?

CORCORAN seems not to hear. Pause.

(slightly louder) Do you want to play Monopoly?

CORCORAN: Eh?

MILLET: Monopoly. Do you want to play Monopoly?

Beat.

CORCORAN: Yeah, alright.

CORCORAN wheels over to the table. MILLET retrieves the board and starts to set it out.

MILLET: You know how to play?

CORCORAN: . . .

MILLET: I used to be really good at Monopoly. Bit of a Monopoly wheeler-dealer, me.

MILLET winces suddenly and rubs its eye.

My bloody eye!

CORCORAN: What's wrong with it?

MILLET: Think I've got something in it. Or both of them.

CORCORAN: Come here, let's have a look.

MILLET: Think I've got an eyelash or something.

CORCORAN: Come here—stop rubbing them—let me have a look.

CORCORAN examines MILLET'*s eyes.*

MILLET: Have I got an eyelash?

CORCORAN: Can't see anything. Bit red, but . . .

MILLET: So bloody itchy.

CORCORAN: Stop rubbing them.

MILLET: But they're so itchy.

MILLET *goes back to sit and set up the board, trying to refrain from rubbing its eyes.*

Doesn't that drive you mad?

CORCORAN: What?

MILLET: Your *(indicates eye)* you know.

CORCORAN: This?

MILLET: Yeah. How'd that happen?

CORCORAN: This?

MILLET: Yeah, how'd it happen?

CORCORAN: Well, when I was a child, about five years old, I wanted to be a ballet dancer . . .

MILLET: Yeah, yeah, alright. Doesn't it drive you mad, though?

CORCORAN: Only itches if I scratch it. Just can't see out of it, that's all.

MILLET: So I suppose your, whatsit, depth perception is buggered.

CORCORAN: Suppose so.

MILLET tuts sympathetically.

So long as I don't have to operate any heavy machinery, I should be alright.

MILLET hands over a wad of Monopoly money to CORCORAN.

MILLET: Can't remember how much we're supposed to start with, but I suppose if we start with the same?

MILLET continues to happily sort out the cards and remaining money, muttering and humming to itself.

CORCORAN looks at the door, FILIGREE's cot.

CORCORAN: What time is it?

MILLET looks at its empty wrist again.

MILLET: (Stupid!)

CORCORAN: Right.

MILLET holds out the dice.

MILLET: Here.

CORCORAN: Eh?

MILLET: You can start.

> *CORCORAN reaches to take the dice. A soft "ding."*

> *MILLET jumps.*

Bloody hell! That—

> *A tray with one bowl—622149 A—appears.*

That thing!

CORCORAN: It's not exactly ear-splitting.

MILLET: No, but it's so quiet and then . . .

> *MILLET makes a shocked, deafened face.*

VOICE: LD50, Stage Two commencing.

> *Another "ding," and a second bowl appears—816123 E.*
> *CORCORAN stares at the bowls. MILLET goes over to them.*

MILLET: Let's hope it's better than breakfast, eh? What?

> *MILLET notices that there are only two bowls.*

Oh. Yeah.

> *Beat.*

It might be back. You don't know, it might be.

CORCORAN beckons for a bowl.

CORCORAN: Come on, then.

MILLET hands CORCORAN its bowl, retrieves its own bowl, and sits down.

You got the right one?

MILLET: Yeah. See?

MILLET turns the bowl so CORCORAN can see the number— 816123 E.

CORCORAN: Yeah, give that one to me.

MILLET: No.

CORCORAN: Come on, give / it me.

MILLET: No! Why? You've got your own dinner.

CORCORAN: I'll swap you.

MILLET: What?

CORCORAN: Come on, I'll swap you.

MILLET: No! This is my one. That's your one. Why d'you keep trying to steal my bloody dinner!

CORCORAN watches as MILLET starts to eat. MILLET grimaces slightly.

CORCORAN: I like you being here. It's good for Filigree.

MILLET: Could have fooled me.

MILLET nods at the dice.

Go on then. You start.

CORCORAN rolls the dice. Moves the game piece. MILLET looks at where it landed.

Want to buy it?

CORCORAN: Yeah, go on then.

Money and card are exchanged. Lights fade. A product commercial, e.g., Huggies.

Lights rise.

CORCORAN is staring carefully at the Monopoly cards. MILLET's head is on the table. It is snoring gently.

The lights suddenly go out with a heavy thud.

MILLET starts awake. It is drooling and has a card stuck to its face.

MILLET: What's going on?

CORCORAN: Lights out.

MILLET: What's that? What's on my face?

CORCORAN reaches over and peels the card from MILLET's face. Peers at it in the gloom.

CORCORAN: Gas Company. You win.

MILLET: Why's it dark?

CORCORAN: Nighttime.

MILLET: Did this happen before?

CORCORAN: Every now and then.

MILLET: Alrighty then. Night night, sleep tight!

MILLET gets up and smacks its knee on the table in the dark.

CORCORAN: Mind the table.

MILLET faces a dilemma about which cot to take.

Take whichever one you want.

MILLET goes to FILIGREE's cot.

Not that one.

MILLET goes to CORCORAN's cot, pauses.

MILLET: What about you?

CORCORAN: I'm fine.

MILLET: Come on, I can help you get in.

CORCORAN: No, really, I'm / alright here.

MILLET wheels CORCORAN to the cot and starts to grapple with it, trying to help it from the chair to the cot, over CORCORAN's protestations.

MILLET: No, come on, you / ought to go to bed.

CORCORAN: Seriously! / I'm alright in my chair!

MILLET: Come on / then.

CORCORAN: I want to sleep in / my chair—

MILLET: You'll get / bed sores or something—

CORCORAN: I always / sleep in my chair—

MILLET: Chair sores / come on, up we go—

CORCORAN: Get off / me, will you?

MILLET: Up / we go—

CORCORAN: Ow!

MILLET: Sorry—

CORCORAN: That's / my—

MILLET: Sorry—

CORCORAN: Put me down, alright? Put me down!

MILLET does.

MILLET: Sorry.

CORCORAN: I said!

MILLET: Sorry.

Beat.

CORCORAN: Just . . .

MILLET: Sorry.

Pause.

MILLET gets into bed. CORCORAN is still right there.

Are you going to sleep in your chair right there?

CORCORAN moves away.

I mean, I don't mind—just . . .

Pause.

Ni' night, then. Sleep tight.

Lights fade.

A commercial, e.g., Iams.

Lights pulse up to blue-out.

CORCORAN sits in its chair beside FILIGREE's cot. MILLET lies in bed. Sighs heavily.

I can't sleep.

MILLET sighs again. Turns over loudly.

CORCORAN: Do your Fibonacci thing.

MILLET: Eh?

CORCORAN: Do your Fibonacci numbers thing. Help you fall asleep.

Beat.

MILLET: Zero, one, one, two, three, five, eight, thirteen, / twenty-one—

CORCORAN: In your head.

MILLET: Oh.

MILLET starts out whispering, not coherently. Coughs slightly.

Lights fade.

Fractured commercials.

Lights pulse back to blue-out.

MILLET is asleep. CORCORAN sits in its chair beside FILIGREE's cot. MILLET coughs violently for a moment.

Lights out again.

Fractured commercials.

Lights up to blue out.

MILLET is still asleep. CORCORAN dozes in its chair.

Door opens. FILIGREE enters and stands in the dark, shivering. It is dripping wet.

The lights come on with a heavy thud. CORCORAN snorts awake. Sees FILIGREE.

CORCORAN: Where's your towel?

FILIGREE: Lost it.

CORCORAN: You going to stand there dripping all day? Come on. Take that stuff off.

FILIGREE comes in, cautiously. Goes behind the cot.

FILIGREE: Don't watch me—it's private.

CORCORAN: Where did you learn that? "Private" . . .

FILIGREE: You. In Primary Socialization.

CORCORAN: Primary Socialization, right. Well-remembered.

CORCORAN studiously turns away while FILIGREE takes off its wet things behind the shelter of the cot's headboard.

What's the world coming to, eh? Sending you back like that.

CORCORAN pulls the sheet off the cot and holds it out to FILIGREE without looking. FILIGREE wraps the sheet around itself like a blanket. Emerges, still shivering.

Come here then.

CORCORAN reaches for FILIGREE, who backs away sharply.

Come on.

FILIGREE allows CORCORAN to vigorously rub its arms and shoulders, trying to get it warm.

. . . sending you swimming in the middle of the bloody night . . .

FILIGREE: Wasn't swimming. I was sat on a stool in the middle of the water. Every time I fell asleep I fell in.

Pause.

CORCORAN: . . . sending you back like this . . .

Pause. FILIGREE reaches out and gently touches the side of CORCORAN's bad eye.

FILIGREE: Corcoran oh Corcoran . . . what was its name?

CORCORAN: I've told you her name, Filigree.

FILIGREE: I like how you say it.

Beat.

CORCORAN: Alice.

FILIGREE explores the scar with unusual tenderness, perhaps strokes CORCORAN's face.

FILIGREE: Poor Alice. Poor little Alice.

CORCORAN: Alright—leave off now.

FILIGREE points at MILLET.

FILIGREE: Something's coming out of its face.

CORCORAN looks over. MILLET *has a nosebleed.*

CORCORAN: (Shit.) Millet. Millet!

MILLET *wakes, groggy.*

MILLET: What? Is it breakfast?

MILLET *sits up. Blood gushes down its face.*

What's—oh! Oh, shit!

CORCORAN: You've got a nosebleed.

MILLET: Yeah, I can see that. Oh (fuck)—

CORCORAN: Could you get out of the bed?

MILLET: Yeah, yeah, sorry. Oh . . .

MILLET *gets up out of bed.*

. . . ah, this is horrible.

MILLET *tips its head back.*

CORCORAN: Don't—don't tip your head back. Tip it forward—

MILLET: Forward?!

CORCORAN: Yeah, and pinch your nose shut.

MILLET: *(doing so)* Yeah? Now what?

CORCORAN: Stay like that.

MILLET: Oh, very funny.

CORCORAN: Should stop it.

MILLET: Meantime I walk about holding my nose like a tit.

    FILIGREE giggles.

You're back, I see.

(to CORCORAN) Why's it got no clothes on?

CORCORAN: Been swimming.

MILLET: Look at this mess.

    A soft "ding."

VOICE: Cleanup in Room Five.

    Another "ding" and a cloth appears, as well as fresh clothes for
    FILIGREE. MILLET retrieves the cloth and tries to clean up its face.
    It sits down rather hard in a chair as it does.

CORCORAN: Could you pass the . . . ?

MILLET: Oh. Sorry.

    MILLET takes FILIGREE's clothes over, then sits down again.

CORCORAN: You alright? You've gone a bit of a funny colour.

MILLET: Never been much good with the sight of blood. Least I'll get a shower in a minute.

CORCORAN: You had your shower already.

MILLET: Seriously? Oh, that's brilliant. Tell you what, next time you have to go swimming, I'll volunteer, alright?

CORCORAN: You don't know how to swim.

MILLET: That's not the point.

FILIGREE: Wasn't swimming. I was sat on a stool in the middle of the water and when I fell asleep I fell in.

MILLET: What's the point of that?

FILIGREE shrugs.

You know, I remember this kid, once, it was really cold out and . . .

Beat. MILLET laughs.

I forgot what I was going to say.

FILIGREE: Was it a story?

MILLET: Might've been, can't remember now. Look at this mess! Ah, well, least I'll get a shower in a minute.

Beat.

A soft "ding"—two bowls appear.

VOICE: LD50, Stage Three commencing.

Another bowl appears.

MILLET experimentally releases its nose, finds it's stopped bleeding, and finishes cleaning up its face while CORCORAN and FILIGREE get their bowls. MILLET gets its bowl and they all start to eat. MILLET stops after one bite.

MILLET: This tastes different. It's like . . .

MILLET considers, then examines the side of the bowl.

Hey! You! Give me my bloody breakfast! I'm not stupid—I can read. Give it.

CORCORAN reluctantly hands over the bowl and takes its own in exchange. MILLET glares at the other two suspiciously.

Why do you always want my food? What's wrong with *your* food?

CORCORAN: Nothing.

MILLET: Stop trying to take my food then. Alright? Just stop it.

They eat in silence for a moment. CORCORAN watches MILLET.

What are you staring at?

CORCORAN: (Nothing.)

CORCORAN retrieves the crossword. FILIGREE licks the bowl, starts chewing the sides.

You'll break your teeth.

FILIGREE stops. Continues with a vengeance.

Filigree!

> *FILIGREE stops. Pause. FILIGREE starts rubbing its back violently against the bed frame.*

"Very sad unfinished story"—oi! Stop. You'll pull your stitches out. You *trying* to get up my nose this morning?

> *CORCORAN returns to the crossword.*

"Very sad unfinished story about rising smoke."

> *MILLET makes a face to FILIGREE, mouthing, "You'll pull your stitches out, meh meh meh." FILIGREE grins. CORCORAN glances up—MILLET resumes an expression of innocence.*

MILLET: How many letters?

CORCORAN: Eight.

FILIGREE: What's happening next door?

MILLET: Don't know.

> *MILLET starts to climb up on the cabinet—misses its footing.*

FILIGREE: Careful.

MILLET: I'm alright.

> *MILLET clambers up, peers through. Pause.*

They're playing charades.

> *Pause.*

It's a book.

With increasing volume through the vent:

Three words. Second word . . . small word, small word, um, it . . . of . . . at . . .

FILIGREE: Can they hear you?

MILLET: *(without turning)* Don't think so. Er . . . and . . . in . . . if . . . If! If, that's it, if! So something "if" something.

CORCORAN: Millet.

MILLET: Okay, first word . . .

CORCORAN: Millet!

MILLET turns, seems slightly confused by the room.

They can't hear you.

MILLET: If something.

MILLET blinks and sways a little.

CORCORAN: Think you should come down from there.

MILLET focuses.

MILLET: I'm alright—just a bit dizzy.

MILLET can't figure out how to get down. Eventually manages, awkwardly.

FILIGREE: Come and lie here with me.

MILLET: You're alright. I'll just . . .

MILLET *indicates* CORCORAN*'s cot.*

Do you mind?

CORCORAN: (Be my guest.)

MILLET *climbs into the cot. Takes some deep breaths—its respiration is a little fast and it's trying to slow it down.*

FILIGREE *crosses to* CORCORAN*'s cot with determination.* MILLET *looks panicked.*

MILLET: No. Nononono, what are you—nonono—hey, hey, alright, alright, just—

FILIGREE *climbs onto the cot beside* MILLET *and continues drawing.*

Bloody hell. I thought it was—phew!

MILLET *takes more deep breaths.*

My heart's going like a—like nineteen to the dozen. Bloody hell, it gave me a fright.

CORCORAN: Don't frighten people, Filigree.

FILIGREE *pats* MILLET, *or some other sign of not-entirely-comforting affection.* MILLET *continues to take deep breaths, trying to get its breathing under control, perplexed.*

MILLET: Air must be thin up there or something.

FILIGREE: Millet oh Millet, why would the air be thin?

MILLET: Cos it's high up. I was just joking, cos I was standing on the—
when you go up very high, the air gets thinner. There's less oxygen.
Like, if you go up a mountain or something.

(to CORCORAN) Here, have you ever climbed Mount Everest?

> *Beat.*

CORCORAN: No. Have you?

MILLET: No. No, I don't think so.

FILIGREE: Why would you want to climb a mountain?

MILLET: Because . . . it'd be an achievement, wouldn't it?

FILIGREE: Of what?

MILLET: Of . . . getting to the top of something really high?

> MILLET *starts to laugh.*

It's really stupid. What a stupid thing to do.

CORCORAN: Does sound like a lot of work for a bit of a view.

FILIGREE: Corcoran oh Corcoran . . .

CORCORAN: Here we go . . .

FILIGREE: Tell us the tale of the time you climbed the mountain.

CORCORAN: Not now.

FILIGREE: Please?

MILLET: Yeah yeah yeah, let's have a story.

CORCORAN: Not now, / come on.

MILLET: A story a story, we want a story.

FILIGREE & MILLET: A story, a story, we want a story!

A soft "ding."

CORCORAN: Saved by the bell.

VOICE: 622149 E.

Beat.

MILLET: That's you, isn't it?

Beat.

CORCORAN: Yep.

Beat. CORCORAN goes to exit.

FILIGREE: But the story.

CORCORAN: Don't kill each other.

FILIGREE: Rrrarrghhh!

FILIGREE launches itself at MILLET.

MILLET cringes back, panicked. FILIGREE laughs. MILLET glares at it. CORCORAN exits.

MILLET: You've got to work on your sense of humour. My heart.

FILIGREE: Can I feel it?

MILLET: No.

FILIGREE tries anyway.

No! It's like you were raised by wolves.

FILIGREE: I don't understand.

MILLET: Doesn't matter. / You just—

FILIGREE: I wasn't raised by anything—why would I be raised by wolves?

MILLET: You weren't raised by anything?

FILIGREE: Corcoran said there's another one like me, but it was put in a family, and got a bedroom and socks and Christmas.

MILLET: Another one just like you?

FILIGREE: Mm-hm. Put in a family, to see what difference it would make.

Beat.

Do you want to see my pictures?

MILLET: Yeah, alright.

FILIGREE *opens the sketch pad and hands it over.* MILLET *looks through.*

Mm. Okay. Wow.

FILIGREE: That's you.

MILLET: That's me, is it? Where's my arms and legs?

FILIGREE: I cut them off.

MILLET: You cut them off.

FILIGREE: *(a trifle guilty)* Yes?

Beat. MILLET *continues.*

MILLET: Right . . . and who's that, then?

FILIGREE: You.

MILLET: Where's my head?

FILIGREE *shrugs.*

You cut it off, didn't you?

FILIGREE *shrugs, nods. Beat.* MILLET *continues.*

FILIGREE: Look, there's you.

MILLET: Oh, that's me as well, is it?

FILIGREE: And you're not cut in pieces in that one.

Beat.

MILLET: What's that thing coming out my chest?

FILIGREE: You have been impaled on a tree.

Beat.

MILLET: Well, these are . . . they're lovely. Thank you for showing them to me.

> MILLET *hands the sketch pad back to a beaming* FILIGREE, *delighted by the praise.*

FILIGREE: What's happening next door?

MILLET: I don't know. You look.

> FILIGREE *scampers over to the cabinet, climbs up, and looks through the air vent.* MILLET *takes a couple of experimental deep breaths. On the second, it starts to cough. Coughs hard into its hand, then peeks at the contents. Is disgusted and perturbed. Surreptitiously wipes it under the pillow.*

FILIGREE: One of them's playing cards, I think. The other one's sleeping.

MILLET: Just two.

FILIGREE: Mm-hm. No, here's the other one.

> FILIGREE *giggles.*

MILLET: What's funny?

FILIGREE: It's got funny bandages on its ears. Looks funny. Like—

FILIGREE cups its ears and does a silly voice.

"I got no ears; I got funny bandage ears; lookit my funny bandage ears."

FILIGREE does a little bandage-ears dance on top of the cabinet.

MILLET laughs. Then coughs again. FILIGREE's expression suddenly changes.

You smell funny.

MILLET: Oh, not this again.

FILIGREE: You do, you smell funny.

MILLET: Well, there's nothing I can do about it.

FILIGREE gets a twinge of itchiness and starts twisting to scratch its back. Rubs it against the edge of the cabinet.

Oi. Oi! Stop that.

FILIGREE: But it's so itchy.

MILLET: Come here. Come here—let me have a look.

MILLET lifts FILIGREE's shirt.

This dressing's disgusting. Look, if I take it off, you've got to promise me you won't scratch. Alright? If you scratch it, the stitches'll break and all your insides will fall out.

FILIGREE looks delighted.

That's not a good thing.

> *MILLET peels off the dressing, making a moue of distaste.*
> *FILIGREE twists and tries to scratch the wound—MILLET slaps its*
> *hand away.*

Oi! What did I just say? Okay, look—maybe I can scratch it for you,
yeah? Really carefully so I don't wreck the stitches. Yeah?

> *MILLET goes to scratch FILIGREE's back. FILIGREE arches away.*

FILIGREE: Your hands are cold!

MILLET: Sorry.

FILIGREE: They're all blue.

MILLET: Just a bit cold.

> *FILIGREE reaches out and rubs MILLET's arms and shoulders,*
> *rather awkwardly, as CORCORAN did earlier. MILLET endures this*
> *treatment for a moment.*

Thank you. Thank you, that's lovely. That's enough, now. Alright?
That's enough, thank you.

FILIGREE: All warm now?

MILLET: All warm now, yes. Thank you.

> *FILIGREE turns abruptly and presents its back to MILLET again.*
> *MILLET scratches carefully.*

That alright?

FILIGREE: Yeah.

A pause while FILIGREE *enjoys its back-scratch.*

I'm very charming, aren't I.

MILLET: Yes, you're very charming.

FILIGREE: Corcoran said things like me are often charming.

MILLET: How does Corcoran know?

FILIGREE: Corcoran used to make things like me.

MILLET: It used to be (one of them out there)? So what's it doing in here?

FILIGREE: It did a wrong thing.

MILLET: That's too bad—what did it do?

FILIGREE: It had a wrong baby. It knew the baby wouldn't be able to pass the Eye. So it tried to hide the baby away. So now it's here.

MILLET: What happened to the baby?

FILIGREE: Got put in a cage in the dark.

MILLET: That's too bad.

FILIGREE: Same as me.

MILLET: (Explains a lot.) So you've never seen outside then? Like, grass and sky and stuff?

FILIGREE: "The Scroobious Pip went out one day
When the grass was green, and the sky was grey.
Then all the beasts in the world came round"

MILLET & FILIGREE: "When the Scroobious Pip sat down on the ground.
The cat and the dog and the kangaroo
The sheep and the cow and the guineapig too—
The wolf he howled, the horse he neighed
The little pig squeaked and the donkey brayed—"

Both are delighted.

MILLET: My mum used to say that poem to me—did yours?

FILIGREE: I don't have a mum.

MILLET: Yeah, my mum used to say that one to me all the time. She
read me poems and stories all the time when I was little, did yours?

FILIGREE: I don't have a mum.

MILLET: Right! Right.

FILIGREE: Corcoran tells me stories.

MILLET: Right. Do you know—oh! I should read you my favourite one!

MILLET gets up with purpose.

I bet I've still got it here somewhere, I wouldn't have—

Looks around, confused.

Where's my . . . (stuff)? Where's . . .

Beat. MILLET *nervous, embarrassed.*

Forgot—forgot where I was.

Pause.

FILIGREE: You smell funny.

MILLET: Well, I'm sure I'll get my shower soon. Shower before break-fast, right?

Uncertain beat. FILIGREE *starts rubbing* MILLET's *arms again, considering this a catch-all solution.*

Yeah, alright, thank you. Thank you. Yeah, stop it. Stop it. Thank you. I'm just going to have a little lie-down, alright? Can I have the—

MILLET *tugs at the blanket.*

Thank you.

MILLET *tucks itself in. Coughs, rubs its eyes.*

FILIGREE: Do you want to play charades?

MILLET: What?

FILIGREE: Do you want to play charades?

MILLET: Do I want to? Do you know how to play charades?

FILIGREE *shrugs.*

FILIGREE: Corcoran said you shouldn't go to sleep in the day. / Because—

MILLET: It'll make my nights very long, yeah. I'm not going to sleep—I'm just going to lie here for a bit, okay? And get warm. I'm bloody freezing.

FILIGREE reaches to rub MILLET again.

NO! No, that's fine, thank you, I've got this blanket.

FILIGREE: I could draw a picture of you.

MILLET: Boiling in acid? On fire?

FILIGREE: No. No, I'll draw it nice. I'll draw you happy.

FILIGREE starts to sketch MILLET. After a moment, it starts to sing its "funny bandage ears" song again.

Lights fade. A commercial.

Lights rise.

FILIGREE is curled around MILLET.

The door hisses open and CORCORAN enters. Its good eye is now freshly burned, red, weeping, and blind.

CORCORAN carefully negotiates its way into the room. Smacks into the corner of the cot. FILIGREE and MILLET both wake with a start. FILIGREE bounces from the cot at the sight of CORCORAN. Throughout the ensuing action, MILLET's cough, eye-rubbing, and high respiratory rate continue and slowly worsen.

CORCORAN: (Ow.)

MILLET: I wasn't asleep . . .

FILIGREE: The story, the story! What's wrong with your face?

MILLET: What—? Oh. Oh, my god, that's horrible.

FILIGREE: Where's your eye gone?

MILLET: Oh. Oh, that's horrible, that is *horrible*, that is.

CORCORAN: Thanks.

FILIGREE experimentally pokes it. CORCORAN jerks away.

MILLET: Can you see anything?

CORCORAN: No.

MILLET: You should put something on it. Ointment or something.

FILIGREE pokes it again. CORCORAN slaps at its hand.

CORCORAN: Oi! Remember when we talked about things hurting?

MILLET: So you can't see anything at all?

CORCORAN: (No.)

FILIGREE looks at MILLET, grins, makes a threatening poking motion again.

MILLET: (Don't!) Hey. Hey—here you go.

MILLET fetches CORCORAN's crossword, presses it and then a pen into CORCORAN's hands.

There you go. Take your mind off it.

CORCORAN: Thank you.

MILLET gets back onto the cot. FILIGREE joins it. CORCORAN just sits. A longish pause.

Do you think you could . . . could you read a clue out for me?

MILLET: Yeah. Oh, yeah, of course, totally.

MILLET goes and peers over CORCORAN's shoulder.

Er, let's see. Alright, um, okay, eight down—"Not seeing window covering"—five letters.

MILLET goes and sits down.

CORCORAN: You're gonna have to . . .

CORCORAN holds up the pen and crossword.

MILLET: Right. Yeah, right, sorry.

MILLET retrieves the crossword and pen from CORCORAN, returns to the cot, and waits for the answer. CORCORAN sits and thinks. It seems slightly at a loss as to what to do with its hands.

Do you want your carrot?

CORCORAN: Eh?

MILLET: Your carrot. Do you want to hold your carrot?

Beat.

CORCORAN: Yeah, alright.

MILLET gets the carrot from under the pillow and takes it to CORCORAN.

MILLET: There you go.

CORCORAN: Thanks.

MILLET returns to the cot.

MILLET: Alright. "Not seeing window covering"—five letters.

MILLET looks at CORCORAN expectantly. Beat.

CORCORAN: Blind.

Beat. FILIGREE starts to giggle. Starts rolling around laughing and pointing at CORCORAN's face.

MILLET: You're a little monster, you are.

FILIGREE: But I'm charming!

MILLET: Charming little monster.

MILLET gives a small laugh, which turns into a cough—it goes and pours itself some water.

CORCORAN: It's a delight to bring such amusement.

MILLET: It's a monster.

FILIGREE: I'm a charming little monster! I'm a charming little monster! I got funny bandage ears, I got—hey, Corcoran, do you want to see my bandage ears dance?

CORCORAN: Yes, Filigree, show me your bandage ears dance.

FILIGREE: No, I said do you want to *see* my bandage ears dance?

Beat.

CORCORAN: Yes, Filigree, I would like to *see* your bandage ears dance, but I'm afraid I won't be able to.

FILIGREE: Why not?

CORCORAN: Because I'm blind.

FILIGREE: Blind! I got funny bandage ears, I got funny bandage ears—

FILIGREE *keeps singing.*

CORCORAN: What have you two been doing?

MILLET: I told it to work on its sense of humour.

CORCORAN: Wonderful.

FILIGREE: Do you want to *see* my drawings, Corcoran?

CORCORAN: Yes, Filigree, I would like to *see* your drawings, but I'm afraid I won't be able to.

FILIGREE: Why not?

CORCORAN: Because I'm / blind—

FILIGREE: Blind! I got funny bandage ears, I got / funny bandage ears—

CORCORAN: Okay, okay, that's enough.

(to MILLET) You doing aerobics or something?

> *FILIGREE pokes at CORCORAN's eye again, repeatedly. CORCORAN slaps its hand away.*

MILLET: Air must be a bit thin. My heart's going like—

> *MILLET puts its fingers to its throat, stares at its bare wrist.*

CORCORAN: Oi! Enough! Enough now! *Enough!*

> *It catches FILIGREE's wrist and grips it.*

This is not allowed.

> *Silence, except for MILLET's breathing.*

Remember what you say.

FILIGREE: Kindness is my friend.

> *FILIGREE carefully kisses CORCORAN's head, hard.*

CORCORAN: Yeah, alright. Alright, you little monster, go and do your drawings.

MILLET: *(realizing)* I think I lost my watch.

> *Beat.*

FILIGREE: Corcoran oh Corcoran, where is your eye?

MILLET: Where would I have left it?

CORCORAN: Not / now.

MILLET: I was sure I was wearing one, *always* wear a watch—where / would I have left it?

FILIGREE: Corcoran oh / Corcoran—

MILLET: Here, neither of you's got a watch, have you?

FILIGREE: —tell us the tale of what / happened to your eye!

MILLET: But I need to check! I need to check my—the—

CORCORAN: Not now, / my love, please . . .

MILLET: —my the time!

FILIGREE: A story, a story!

MILLET: What if I'm late? / Eh?

FILIGREE: A story, a story!

MILLET: What if I'm—I'll miss / breakfast!

FILIGREE: A story, a story! We want a story!

> MILLET *rubs its eyes frantically.* FILIGREE *hops about joyously, pointing from* MILLET *to* CORCORAN *and back.*

Blind and blind and blind and / blind—

MILLET: I'm not—I'm not bloody blind, I'm—could you see if there's something in them?

CORCORAN: I'd like to see if there's something in them, but I'm afraid I won't be able to.

FILIGREE sings quietly, but with gusto, like a child.

FILIGREE: Blind! I got / funny bandage ears—

MILLET: Right. Right, I'm sorry. I'm sorry. It's alright—I'll get my shower in a minute. I can wash it out. Whatever it is. Is the air really thin or something? Is the . . .

MILLET sits down hard. Breathing is difficult.

CORCORAN: Really sorry, Millet.

MILLET: You can't help it. You can't help being blind. It's alright, I'm going swimming in a minute, I can wash it out. I remember there was this kid, one time, it was cold out, and it went swimming—it was still a he—he went swimming except he fell through the ice. That's stupid, isn't it? That's stupid. Climbing a mountain, that's stupid. I never climbed a mountain. The air would be thin. I'm not stupid. I'm not stupid . . .

MILLET tries to get up—the struggle is loud enough that CORCORAN can hear it.

CORCORAN: What are you doing?

MILLET: What's happening next door?

CORCORAN: Nothing.

MILLET: Am I supposed to go next door? I don't want to be late for / the story—

CORCORAN: Millet, sit down.

MILLET: For the—for the stor—late for the—I'm late, I'm late—that's the one! That's the one my mum! Oh my ears and whiskers, he says, oh my ears / and whiskers—

CORCORAN: Hey, Millet—

MILLET: Oh, my ears / and whiskers—

CORCORAN: Millet, Filigree's never seen you do your Fibonacci thing.

MILLET: My?

CORCORAN: I bet Filigree would like to see you do your Fibonacci thing. With the numbers.

MILLET: I would like Filigree to see me do my numbers but I'm afraid I cannot because I am blind.

FILIGREE & MILLET: Blind! I got funny bandage ears, I got / funny bandage ears!

MILLET breaks down coughing, tries to breathe.

CORCORAN: Filigree, wouldn't you like to see Millet do its numbers?

FILIGREE nods.

MILLET: Okay. Okay. Okay. Okay.

CORCORAN: Come on. Zero. One.

MILLET: Zero, one. One. Two. Three.

CORCORAN: Five. / Five.

MILLET: Five. Eight. Eight. Eight, I'm late I'm late I'm late—

CORCORAN: Come on, don't get stuck. Eight, thir/teen . . .

MILLET: I'mlatethirteen. Twenty-one. Twenty one jack queen king, jack / queen king—

CORCORAN: Focus, my love.

MILLET: Jackqueenking, oh my ears / and whiskers—

CORCORAN: Twenty-one, twenty / one—

MILLET: —twenty ears and whiskers, I'm late I'm late I'm late—

MILLET degenerates into a coughing fit, fighting to breathe.

CORCORAN: Get it some water, my love.

FILIGREE goes to fetch some water as MILLET fights back the cough.

MILLET: Too late to say hello goodbye, I'm late I'm la—

More coughing. FILIGREE brings a cup of water to MILLET. Holds its head and helps it drink a little.

Pause.

MILLET seems to have the cough under control. Clings to FILIGREE, taking quick shallow breaths through its nose.

Its body is suddenly racked with another bout of coughing, and a gout of blood flies from its mouth.

It collapses, fighting for breath with its hemorrhaging lungs. This continues for some time. FILIGREE *watches, thoughtful, with some concern.*

FILIGREE: Shall I kill it?

CORCORAN: No, my love.

FILIGREE: But kindness is my friend.

CORCORAN: It's not allowed.

FILIGREE watches. MILLET *dies.*

Silence. A soft "ding."

VOICE: LD50 complete.

Pause. FILIGREE *examines it cautiously.*

FILIGREE: I think its insides came out.

Perplexed, FILIGREE *pats its head. Then rubs its shoulders with increasing vigour. No response.*

CORCORAN: Put it at the door. Put it at the door, or the cleaners will have to come in and get it.

FILIGREE drags MILLET's body to the door. The door opens. MILLET's *body is dragged swiftly out. The door closes. Beat.*

FILIGREE hops up on the cabinet, looks through the air vent.

FILIGREE: Two now.

CORCORAN: Do your drawings.

FILIGREE goes to its book. Watches CORCORAN thoughtfully for a moment.

FILIGREE: Corcoran oh Corcoran? Will you tell me the tale of what happened to your eye?

Beat.

CORCORAN: When I was a little child, just little, just about five years old, I decided that when I grew up I wanted to be . . .

FILIGREE: An astronaut.

CORCORAN: An astronaut? Alright. I decided I wanted to be an astronaut. Do you know what an astronaut does?

FILIGREE: No.

CORCORAN: Then why'd you say it? Okay, I wanted to be an astronaut, who goes up in space, and gets to walk on the moon and collect stars and bring them home as Christmas presents. I thought about being an astronaut all day and every day, and dreamed about it at night. So one day, when I / was old enough—

A soft "ding."

VOICE: 455743 E.

FILIGREE hops up happily, kisses CORCORAN *on the head.*

FILIGREE: Tell me the rest when I get back. Think of good stuff!

FILIGREE exits.

CORCORAN *sits for a moment. Slowly unwraps its carrot and eats it. Lights fade.*

ad copy

These are the original audio jingles / ad copy written for the Toronto production. If pre-existing product commercials are used instead, please ensure they are for products that are still tested on animals, or from companies that exhibit disregard for humane treatment of animals.

Youthanize Face Cream

Your face.

Your face is your beauty. Your face is your life.

Don't lose your life to unnecessary signs of aging—take back your youth with Youthanize—the revolutionary new essential face cream from Lazarus Studios. Infused with active naturals designed to fight signs of aging, Youthanize uses radical revivifying ingredients clinically proven to give you a better life.

Take back your face. Take back your life with Youthanize!

Lazarus—you're all that matters.

Get Lucky! Mascara

Life's a lottery! That guy! That promotion! Those cool new friends! How you gonna get 'em? By getting lucky!

Start winning at life with Get Lucky! Mascara, the dazzling new formula from Elysium!

No clumping! No flaking! Just sensational lashes that are four times thicker! Six times longer! And one thousand times luckier! Smash through that glass ceiling! Marry the man of your dreams!

Start winning at life with Get Lucky! Mascara. Elysium—be all you can be.

Slam! Body Spray

What kind of man are you?

What kind of woman do you want?

What kind of man does the woman you want her to be want you to be?

Man up with Slam! Body Spray! Now in three fresh scents—Tropical Avalanche, Arctic Gorilla, and Gunmetal Storm.

Be strong. Be a man with Slam! Body Spray. Slam!—be the man she wants you to be.

Mamma Huggin's Chicken Shack

Come on down to Mamma Huggin's Chicken Shack! Delicious all-white meat chicken strips, chicken nuggets, chicken poppers, popcorn chicken, chicken-fried steak, pork-fried chicken, chicken chicken cheap cheap cheap chicken, and don't miss our all new finger-lickin' Southern fried chicken bucket—five bucks five bucks five bucks! Come on down to Mamma Huggin's for a tasty taste of the homestead!

Sung: "Cheap cheap cheap! Cheap cheap chicken!"

ZipZap Cleaning Wipes

Breakfast spills or messy after-school snacks! Fun in the garden or baking with Grandma! Wholesome family activities that all have one thing in common—GERMS!

Keep your loved ones safe from harm with ZipZap disposable multi-surface cleaning wipes—laboratory tested to be safe for your whole family to use, ZipZap eradicates germs and keeps your home ZipZap clean!

Make your home a sparkling paradise with ZipZap multi-surface cleaning wipes. ZipZap—for a brighter, better tomorrow!

Happy Snuggles Diapers

Your baby is a little monkey, always busy, always active, learning, playing—she doesn't have time for poopies!

Lil Scramblers diapers from Happy Snuggles BumBum Care give your little angel all the protection she needs, with comfy elasticated leg holes to prevent leaks, and special wicking fabric to keep those oopsies away from her precious skin, so that she can be the happy, perfect baby you want her to be.

> *Sung: "Bum Bum, Bum Bum, Happy Snuggles Bum Bum Care."*

Optional tag: For perfect babies.

PanaNostra

Is life getting you down? Are you plagued by headaches, depression? Is joint pain making life a misery? Do you have digestive issues, sinusitis, shingles, gout?

Talk to your health-care professional about PanaNostra. PanaNostra relieves the discomfort of multiple conditions and helps you get back to the great life you deserve to lead.

(PanaNostra can cause unwanted side effects such as swollen limbs, hair loss, liver failure, epidermal rash, internal bleeding, suicidal thoughts or actions. If these symptoms persist, consult your doctor or pharmacist.)

PanaNostra—get back to being you.

acknowledgements

Many thanks to The Maggie Tree, Kristi Hansen, Vanessa Sabourin, Dr. Michelle Jendral, Mark Meer, Raymond and Gail Cornish, Peta Cornish, Stewart Lemoine, the Varscona Theatre, Nancy McAlear, Coal Mine Theatre, Ted Dykstra, Diana Bentley, and Rae Ellen Bodie.

Belinda is an actor and playwright. Her last two plays, *Little Elephants* and *Category E*, both received Elizabeth Sterling Haynes Awards for Outstanding New Play. She is a core company member of Die-Nasty, the live improvised soap opera, a member of the acting ensemble with Teatro La Quindicina, and founder of her own company, Bright Young Things. She is the recipient of a Rosie Award and a Canadian Screen Award nomination for her performance in the sitcom *Tiny Plastic Men*, and she voices a variety of characters in BioWare's *Mass Effect* and *Dragon Age* games. She lives in Edmonton in a Halloween house with her husband and two small but mighty dogs.

First edition: April 2019
Printed and bound in Canada by Imprimerie Gauvin, Gatineau

Jacket art by Claire Uhlick

**PLAYWRIGHTS
CANADA PRESS**

202-269 Richmond St. W.
Toronto, ON
M5V 1X1

416.703.0013
info@playwrightscanada.com
www.playwrightscanada.com
@playcanpress